WHERE DO I STAND?

A Perception of Self-Understanding and Living Life

By

Michael B Jones.

DEDICATION

Dedication to the beautiful, responsible, and hardest working woman I have ever known my mother, Earnestine Jones Alexander. This mother was able to program a boy to be a man.

CONTENTS

SEASON CHANGE

Michael B. Jones

The season has arrived to make a change.

Take inventory and decide what to exchange.

Remove those beliefs that have created pain.

Create new thoughts that will help you sustain.

The road to change will be tedious.

You will have to hold on to the reigns of obedience.

The old habit will try to regain its position.

Remember you are in charge you cannot give it permission.

This is the season to make a choice, to take a chance if you want anything to change.

PREFACE

The purpose of this book is to help one to consider their perception of a question that most people ask themselves or might be asked by others, once in a moment or a lifetime. Often, most people find themselves in a situation and wonder to themselves," Which way do I go? What should I do?" It is not because people do not know, it is because people tend to struggle in the process of making decisions that have them torn between what is right and what is wrong or what is good and what is bad. Sometimes life will present situations in which a person will make many decisions and question themselves. I can honestly say that life has many twists and turns, that can be either good or bad, funny, or sad. For many years there have been different people playing puppet masters with the emotions of people and the way people think. I strongly believe that the time has come to put an end to the puppet masters of society. The time has come for people to control their destiny based on what they believe and not because others are pushing their belief system, on them in a manner that can mimic brainwashing. To know where you stand on your own anything you need to have your reasoning and your own perception of life. My prayer is that this book will help guide you to knowing where you stand.

INTRODUCTION

"A knowledge of the interactions of your conscious and subconscious minds will enable you to transform your whole life."

Joseph Murphy

———————◆———————

I have come to realize as I look back over my life, due to the lack of education, I had no clue of how crucial a part the subconscious and conscious minds played in my development as a person and as a man. As far as I was concerned the things that I experienced, were the things I was supposed to go through. Everything I experienced was the determining factor of who and what I was to become.

In the effort to help one understand where one stand, a person must be aware that humans operate on a conscious and subconscious level. The conscious mind includes such things as sensations, perceptions, memories, feelings, and fantasies inside of our current awareness. The subconscious mind stores all of your previous life experiences, <u>your beliefs</u>, your memories, your skills, all situations you've been through, and all images you've ever seen. The conscious generates ideas and impresses those ideas into the subconscious.

"Your subconscious mind does not argue with you. It accepts what your conscious mind decrees. If you say, "I can't afford it," your subconscious mind works to make it true. Select a better thought. The decree, "I'll buy it. I accept it in my mind." Joseph Murphy

For a person to get to a point of comprehension in knowing where they stand, the conscious and the subconscious must work together, as a team, because the desire (conscious) is what gets you going and the habit (subconscious) is what keeps you going.

The conscious mind attributes are: it is the thinking educated mind, that creates the part where our goals, wishes, and desires come from. The conscious mind initiates our voluntary actions, the area where we decide to choose and accept or reject. Short-term memory is the area where our short-term memory operates and that period is about 20 seconds. This area of the mind is time-oriented where it operates in the past and the future. The capacity of short-term memory is limited and it can do one to three events at a time. We operate in the conscious mind for about five percent of the day.

"The key to success is to focus our conscious mind on things we desire not things we fear." Brian Tracy

The subconscious mind attributes: it is the habitual mind which means it learns by repetition. It is the emotional mind where once we get emotionally attached to our thoughts, interactions occur to produce results of our thoughts. The subconscious is designed to protect and keep us safe, and control processes related to the maintenance and sustaining of the physical body (such as blood circulation, breathing, digestion, and body temperature). The subconscious is what tells our body to function. This is the area where your long-term memory resides, the subconscious operates at a high capacity and can do thousands of events at a time, and operates in the present time, operating at ninety-five percent of the day. The subconscious never rests.

"Whatever we plant in our subconscious mind, and nourish with repetition and emotion will one day become reality" Earl Nightingale

CHAPTER 1
WHERE DO I STAND IN MY LIFE?

"Your life does not get better by chance; it gets better by change"

Jim Rohn

To determine where you stand in life, you must know what life is all about. Ask yourself a series of questions: What is life to me? What is life supposed to be? What am I supposed to do with life? What do I want out of life? Once you determine what life is to you and how it goes, then you have an idea of what it will take for a solid foundation. To stand you need solid ground on which to build a solid platform of understanding.

As a youth, the only thing we understood was that if I am breathing, I am living. When we became an adolescent there was the view that our guardian was controlling our lives because we could not do what you wanted to do. We wanted control of our lives, not realizing we had no idea what living life was all about.

Then we started taking matters into our own hands, not understanding the decisions that we were making would affect our lives. The repercussions and consequences would start to set in either good or bad. Once we reach adulthood, this is when life really starts.

What has happened at this point is that from childhood to adulthood our experiences are programmed into our subconscious to develop our character. For some with more positive experiences, we can identify the individuals who seem happy and joyous. The ones with negative experiences, seem meaner and sadder. We should learn to ask ourselves what side of the river we stand on, the positive side or the negative side. Once we identify which one of the sides we are on, this helps to get an understanding of our life. If we happen to be one of the ones that had a positive outlook, then we need to continue to program our subconscious with positive affirmations and thoughts of positivity.

"Positive Thinking Produces Positive Results"

Positive people are not exempt from bad things happening to them, but the magic of having a programmed subconscious with positive thoughts and ideas helps to overcome obstacles and situations that arise in their lives. A positive mindset helps you to climb your mountains. The partner of positive thinking is a positive attitude!

"A powerful attitude awakens inner strength, energy, motivation, and initiative." Remez Sassion

Do all things without grumblings or questions. Philippians 2:14

Always keep in mind that a mountain always rises, and your attitude will determine how fast you get to the top of the mountain.

The most toxic form of the subconscious mind is negative programming. The bad experiences of life have damaged so many individuals whose life encounters of negativity overshadowed their positive encounters. A negative person can live a miserable life for a long time. Individuals who are miserable feel as if it was not for bad luck, it would be no luck, or they can never get a break or anyone like them. Just as in the medical field there are cures for many diseases. The subconscious mind infected with negative thoughts will deteriorate your life. It can cause bad heart conditions, bad headaches, and obesity, there are many issues the body goes through when negativity is the center of your life. The antidote for negativity is to interject positivity. Once you have taken the antidote or had surgery for positivity there is still physical therapy to go through. Physical therapy is a lifelong session done every second, minute, and hour. During these physical therapy sessions whatever negative situations happen, look for the positive. This physical therapy is like the drive to lose weight; you must have the discipline to be healthy. If you have spent much of the time in your life with negative thoughts, you are in the valley, and at the base of your mountain looking up at the mountain and saying," I cannot do this". The positive response to this is to say," I can climb this mountain!" While you are in the valley, and at the base of the mountain making up your mind to climb, remember The Lord is your shepherd, and you lack for nothing. He makes you lie down in your green pastures and he will lead you beside still waters. The Lord is the one who refreshes your soul. He guides you along the right paths of your life for his namesake. Whenever you are in your darkest valley you have no fears because the Lord is with you. The staff and rod of the Lord will comfort you because he is your protector. There is no further need to worry about your enemies. The Lord will prepare your table so that you will live in the presence of them. There will be no longer a need to worry about luck because he will anoint your head with oil and your cup will overflow. You can always be confident that goodness and mercy shall follow you all the days of your life and you will dwell in the house of the Lord forever. As long you seek the kingdom of God, your desires will manifest.

As you think about life there are things to keep in mind: the guarantees are you will live and you will die so do not live in misery but live with vigor and joy.

"Here today gone today."

14

CHAPTER 2
WHERE DO I STAND WITH MY SELF-PRESERVATION?

Self -Preservation (survival) is described as protecting oneself from harm or destruction. Many that are alive want to stay alive. If you think about the things needed to stay physically alive: (oxygen, water, food, and shelter) our mind naturally sends us forth in search of these things. Many individuals go to great lengths to make sure that these needs are met.

The problem is most people do not know how to allow their mental self -preservation (survival) skills to give them a chance to adequately live a life of abundance, prosperity, and wealth. When we reflect on our past childhoods some experiences are rough and some smooth. Remember the need for oxygen, water, food, and shelter provided by the guardian over us whether it was a small or a large quantity. There was someone to provide the things for our physical needs, including the matter of the heart and mind.

Childhood programming was taking place due to their respective environments. As life continues, we find ourselves at a stage where we are filtering through the programming that took place in childhood to make it coincide with the present reality at our point in time. One day you find yourself saying it is not making sense because situations are different. Experiences are changing and we find ourselves processing our memory banks looking for ways to cope and deal with our new situations.

Experiences throughout life change. For instance, when starting elementary school, we are coming from an environment of nurturing and affection to an environment of intimidation and dislike. At home, you were the best and the sweetest now you are in an environment where you might be struggling for that affection and attention that you were accustomed to having. A period has passed and you are acclimated to elementary, now it is time to move on to Middle School.

You advance to Middle School expecting the same set of ideas you experienced in Elementary School. They held your hands, guided you through situations, and you received gold stars! Those were the good old days. When Middle School starts, you must adapt to new classmates, new teachers, and new classwork. Responsibility has become part of your vocabulary. Your mind is flipping out and you are searching for answers to try to figure out what is going on. This would be where you started to utilize the concept of The Law of Nature Self-Preservation (survival). As time passes on, you learn how to adapt to your new experiences, new ideas, and new thought processing. Life for you at this point starts to settle down and then guess what, it is time to go to High School. Emotions increase, you are excited and ready to go because you know what to expect. Once a person has gone through similar experiences their mind is set to survive those familiar experiences.

"Life is a journey with problems to solve lessons to learn but most of all experiences to enjoy".

High School starts and there is a twist. There are some people you know and others you do not know, but you are stable you have experienced this before, so you know how to survive. Suddenly you are exposed to something you have never encountered called. It is called sex, drugs, and alcohol. You are experiencing people who have familiarity with this and now there are new vocabulary word peer pressure, love, and disobedience. Some do overcome and survive; some get bumps and bruises and then some just do not overcome. Survival techniques for most people started in High School, now it is time to face the biggest school of all called LIFE.

Unknown to most people the school of life deals with the positive and negative mindset of your subconscious. Experiences you have encountered from birth to High School graduation were your foundation base. Now things you encountered affected you, what people said to you, and most of all what you said to yourself. As you continue to go through life, your mental survival skills will be tested. If you choose not to expand your positive function of survival and consider letting the negative aspects of your thoughts control you, there is a strong possibility of you asking yourself, "Where do I stand with myself preservation?" The question comes to your mind because you find yourself in the realm of lacking, finding others to justify who you are, and trying to buy love. Others examples are people using you, thoughts of suicide, consumption of drugs, and drinking to numb any pain.

One must keep in mind the energy you put out; is the energy you get back.

"*Life is like a garden you reap what you sow*". *Paulo Coelho*

Life is not respective of energy. Even the positive gets there just through trials and tribulations. The positive has a different means of survival. There are no pity parties and no continuous droughts in life. Love is given regardless of obstacles. Being positive identifies looking for a reason to live. Positivity is the antidote for pain it creates a better way to transmit good vibrations to people you encounter.

"Positive thinking produces positive results".

The time has come for you to go into survival mode to guard your mind against all the negativity that is polluting society. The more you focus on emitting positive energy into the universe, you put yourself in a position to overcome your circumstances. Your perception and understanding would be different from those whom we have in our inner circle.

Step up and take the challenge to put your mind on a diet. Get rid of the negativity that you feed yourself and replenish with positive thoughts that will change your mental self-preservation tremendously.

"You are what you believe you are".

"I have come to believe that caring for myself is not self-indulgent caring for myself is an act of survival ". Audre Lorde

CHAPTER 3

WHERE DO I STAND IN MY STRUGGLES?

Society has painted a picture of the struggle as unhappy, and negative. Just hearing the word struggle, a person's mindset immediately associates negative words or statements such as; having a hard time battling with something or someone troubling, having conflict, and or exerting a lot of effort. If you look at countries around the world and different individuals' lives, that might be going through hardship. Those who stand on the outside looking in will view them as struggling with a situation or obstacle that they cannot overcome. Those who stand on the outside are the ones who have created a picture of struggling, to look at as if there is no hope. So when someone looks out of the window this is the image that brainwashes them, to view their struggle as unhappy or negative. While going through a struggle there is a level of frustration that builds, rendering the ability to think straight. The more you look at the picture, the more your struggle controls your life. This all stems from how the subconscious mind programming was conditioned to view and deal with the concept of struggle.

"Your struggle is your strength if you can resist becoming negative, bitter, or hopeless in time your struggle will give you everything. Bill McGill

In my life, the toughest struggle for me was my identity. There is nothing tougher than growing up not knowing what to be, who to be, or how to be. My time as a child was under the guidance of a single mom. Praise my mother because she knew I was to grow up as a man, but the type of man was unknown. I am the oldest of three, therefore, from my point of view, I was the beginning of my mother's new life experience. My mother was the youngest offspring of her parents. Therefore, having three older brothers and a sister raised in Mississippi (during the fifties and the sixties,) picking cotton was hard work and she knew it well. My mother viewed the men around her as working and caring for their families. Most times people tend to overlook the influence of their childhood when going through struggles. If a person honestly stops and reflects on their childhood with there should be a part of your spirit that shows that you are the way you are because of particulars in your childhood past that will reveal to you why you say what you say, do what you do, and think the way you think. My mother's point of view of a man came from what she experienced before my conception. Therefore, I can say that I do not struggle with the hard work ethic and responsibility aspect of my life. In my opinion, this was my foundation growing up which I have been able to add to and make greater. The ability to create and sustain a family, the strength to be a leader in the workplace, and to evolve to identify my purpose in life.

"Without a solid foundation, you'll have trouble creating anything of value".

Erika Oppenheimer.

Recalling my thoughts of my younger years and my experiences around the many male influences, I understood hard work, taking care of your family, and keeping money in my pocket. I was influenced to keep plenty of women, beginning around the age of 8 years old this was my playbook to manhood. My mother however enforced working hard, being responsible, and doing well in school. The influence from school was to dress nice, be cool, and talk to girls. When people are blind to the dramatic effect of their surroundings, everything they do is perfectly fine from their perspective. Therefore, the things I have done and said before my new programming has been a mixture of helpful and hurtful. During this phase of my life, I realized not only was I hurting others, but I was also hurting myself. There is a universal law called the Law of Cause and Effect. This law states that every single action in the universe produces a reaction no matter what it may be. The issue with my identity struggle was that I was a Quarterback utilizing a playbook that was not designed for me. I did not filter out what was the proper thing for me I took what was programmed in me and started living. Most people have entrusted their future to misinformation instilled in them without questioning it or have chosen to survive in their struggles with tools that are not beneficial, financially, emotionally, physically, or spiritually.

"Life is a matter of choices and every choice you make makes you".

John C. Maxwell

It was at the age of forty -five I started a journey to find my identity. It came about when I choose to earn an Associate's Degree to help propel and advance my career. The course of study was psychology. This course covered the subconscious mind. It educated me on how the subconscious mind takes in everything from birth to your present day, or life moment, where positive or negative information has its effects on a person's life. This effect determines the perspective of what or how someone deals with struggles or choices. Honestly, I was having quite a few suicidal moments because I was not happy in my life. Even though I have a beautiful family, I was not happy with myself, and I did not understand why. I reached my limit of being something or someone I was not. I felt drained and tired, and people were so ungrateful for the hard work I put in to please them, my family, church, and even work (where I found my most fulfillment) in my job started dissipating. The more I researched subconsciousness and consciousness and super-consciousness. More hope started to awaken inside of me. My research showed and encouraged me to reprogram myself. The journey continued, along with the introduction to more information to reinforce my knowledge and help me find the person God created me to be. Along this journey, I found out that I was being a Pretender, not to impress others, but impressing myself. Most people look in the mirror and are dissatisfied with whom they see, so they pretend to be a better version of who is seen. I spent so many years aligning myself with the image of my Influencers and I was not doing what I believed. I was a failure, I put a mask on every time I looked in the mirror and I was not pleased with the reflection looking back at me. Most people, when faced with dissatisfaction, place blame on other areas to avoid dealing with it and that is what I did. Placed the blame on my wife, my church family, and my family. I chose to reprogram my subconscious with positive, and inspirational thoughts, words, and people. It has worked. I know who I am now and when I see my reflection, I am pleased with the outcome.

"Your life does not get better by chance; it gets better by change".

Jim Rohn

Life struggles will always be at the forefront of a person's life. There is a struggle in every category of our lives. The question is how will you handle it or will you mask it up? Will you place the blame on others, or will you search deep down and find a way to combat the pending struggle? The journey I have been on has encouraged me to combat and conquer any struggle that I may be facing at any given moment. Though I do not want to, I chose to stand on the battlefield and go to war with whatever struggle I am faced with. In reflecting on being my mother's firstborn, she instilled that in me, but I did not see it until now. My mother chose to go to war with the struggle of single parenting and she did not mask it. She did not place blame, but chose to stay on the battlefield and conquer it, not once but three times. Past programming had me blaming my mother for the lack thereof, overlooking the key ingredient to life which is evolution without being in fear. The person I was looking for has always been with me but covered up by insignificant things. There will be times when purging the negative inputs from life is necessary to uncover the positive that already exists and make room for new positives that are required to evolve.

"Life is about evolving don't stay in a situation that is not helping you grow mentally, spiritually, and emotionally ".

Author Unknown.

CHAPTER 4
WHERE DO I STAND IN MY FUTURE?

Most people are fact-driven. One fact I have found, to be certain is we will all live and die. The length of time to face these two truths are unknown. Fear of the unknown has stagnated many people. Fear of the unknown has broken so many. Fear of the unknown has blinded others from the pursuit their dreams.

In my High School junior year, I signed up to enlist in the United States Navy under the delayed entry program. This would position me to enter the military right out of high school. I would have to do is sign and give the oath to protect the United States of America to the best of my abilities. The day came and it was time for me to leave at the age of 18 years old. I stood in an airport for the first time in my life (unknown) and had never been on an airplane before(unknown). There was a battle going on inside of me that I had never felt before (unknown). After being accustomed to having direction on what to do and how to do it on a constant basis I now felt abandoned. The only thing communicated to me was to sit here until they say the board and get on the plane. The battle inside of me intensified. My first thought was to become a flight risk (flee) or die. Where are these thoughts coming from? I was programmed as a child that if God wanted me to fly, God would have given me wings. The greatest of them all do not trust planes as they can fall out of the sky. As this extreme conversation was going on in my head, with whom I call me, myself and I, common ground was reached. I honestly reasoned with myself that death is certain. No man knows the day or hour, so we must continue to live. The decision to face the unknown changed my life. Boarding the plane led me to a new adventure in my life, with new experiences, new people, new cultures, and a treasure hunt for a new me. When we go through life fearing the unknown, we go through life and miss living.

"We all have a fear of the unknown what one does with that fear will make all the difference in the world". Lillian Russel

The life we are living is the only one granted. As the world turns there are images of those living good lives, mediocre lives, and not-so-good lives. Unbelievably, life was created to be lived in a good way. However, the good life depends on the person living it. I have been on earth for half of a century and my life, to me, has been a roller coaster ride. There have been some loops, some turns, and even some upside-down maneuvers. Honestly, there has been a mixture of good and bad, happy, and sad as I am sure all of us can relate to. The roller coasters' causes and effects all derived from choices that were made on my part. If you are in a place of negativity sadder than happy get on the plane and travel to a destination of positivity which can generate a process of evolution. During my roller coaster ride I learned that no one can live my life for me, only I can. The different maneuvers of the roller coaster along with other passengers riding will try to manipulate your life in a way they think it should be lived. The choices we choose will border at times of selfishness in my opinion and sometimes a little selfishness is required to evolve.

I grew up in the era when Black/African Americans commonly stated." The white man is holding them down." In my opinion, this statement likely held some truths as we identified opportunities were slower in progress as opposed to our white counterparts. However, me, myself, and I always debated this statement until we came to the realization that life has obstacles in many forms. To live my life, my choice was not to allow the obstacles to deter me from the goals that I had chosen to achieve. When we can face obstacles ahead that is a sign of evolution.

When there is fear of the unknown, this is known as regression. Every battle against an obstacle does not lead to a victory but it leads to experience.

"Pleasant experiences make life delightful. Painful experiences lead to growth".

Anthony De Mello

This life was created to experience everything God has to offer. We are not designed to just exist. We were created to be great in our unique way. The time has come to cut the strings of the puppeteer, get up and make a choice to have more, do better and reward yourself by enjoying life.

"Accept what has happened and deal with the rest". Michael Jones

This quote is my own. I have learned that I cannot change the past. There are things done as we live that cannot be undone. Chose to accept it, embrace it, and live with it knowing the experience of it. "Deal with the rest" motto means your evolution has better prepared you to handle unforeseen issues in a manner that brings more reward and less stress. Every day one must look to move forward to search, and create, new experiences in their life. So, when the time comes to face the last fact (death) you will know that you lived your life your way.

Romans 12:2, <u>NIV</u>: Do not conform to the pattern of this world, but be transformed by the renewing of your mind. Then you will be able to test and approve what God's will is--his good, pleasing and perfect will.

Romans 12:2, <u>ESV</u>: Do not be conformed to this world, but be transformed by the renewal of your mind, that by testing you may discern what is the will of God, what is good and acceptable and perfect.

Romans 12:2, <u>NASB</u>: And do not be conformed to this world, but be transformed by the renewing of your mind, so that you may prove what the will of God is, that which is good and acceptable and perfect.

Romans 12:2, <u>NLT</u>: Don't copy the behavior and customs of this world, but let God transform you into a new person by changing the way you think. Then you will learn to know God's will for you, which is good and pleasing and perfect.

Romans 12:2, <u>CSB</u>: Do not be conformed to this age, but be transformed by the renewing of your mind, so that you may discern what is the good, pleasing, and perfect will of God.

Romans 12:2, <u>KJV</u>: And be not conformed to this world: but be ye transformed by the renewing of your mind, that ye may prove what is that good, and acceptable, and perfect, will of God.

Where Do I Stand ?????????

Make the choice, to take the chance, if you want anything to change.

GOD BLESS.

Made in the USA
Monee, IL
07 July 2026

56551788R00022